THE WORLD OF THE BRITISH MUSEUM

Clio Whittaker

CONTENTS

NORTH AMERICA

EUROPE

Rome Greece

CENTRAL ASIA

Korea Japan

Atlantic Ocean

Mesopotamia
NEAR EAST

China

Egypt

SOUTH ASIA

SOUTH EAST ASIA

Pacific Ocean

AFRICA

India

SOUTH AMERICA

Indian Ocean

AUSTRALIA

Welcome to The British Museum!

This book will introduce you to the kinds of things you will see in this famous museum. In order to give you an idea of the enormous range of the collections, each double-page spread concentrates on a particular period or part of the world and may cover several galleries or departments in the museum.

> **Use the border colours to help find the right galleries on the map.**

The selection of objects exhibited is always changing, so some of the things illustrated here may not be on display when you visit. However, there are over 50,000 exhibits at any one time, so you can be sure that there will always be more than enough to see!

The six million objects in the amazing treasure-house that is the British Museum cover thousands of years of human history and come from all parts of the globe. But they all have one thing in common: every single object can tell us something about the way of life and beliefs of the people who made it.

In the British Museum you can find out what people ate in ancient Egypt or learn about the Japanese way of painting. You can investigate how the Romans decorated their homes or see what Palestinians wear on special occasions. You can discover how the Aztecs worked out the date, or see how religions crossed the globe. You can study the development of writing, or compare the weapons used by people in the Pacific islands and ancient Rome. It is not surprising that people sometimes find it difficult to know where to begin!

Marble statue of Demeter
350–330 BC
Found in the Sanctuary of Demeter at Knidos

Demeter is shown seated on a throne. The lower arms are lost, as are the hands, one of which probably held a libation bowl or torch. The head was carved separately from the body. The goddess is portrayed as a model of Greek womanhood, serene, mature, motherly and modestly veiled.

Gr 1859.11-26.26 (Sculpture 1300)

Bronze figure of a dancing man
2nd–1st century BC

Payne Knight Bequest
GR 1824.4-31.6

Every object on display has a label with information about where and when it was made. Can you work out how objects came to the Museum? Each label also shows the unique Museum number that identifies the object.

Where do I start in the Museum?

You could start your visit by going to the Information Desk, where the staff will be able to tell you about activities, gallery trails and special events that are suitable for your age and interests. Many activities take place in the Clore Education Centre, which contains the Young Visitors' Centre. Booked school groups can use these facilities to eat packed lunches and families can also drop in, if space is available. Or you could go straight to the Annenberg Information Centre in the Reading Room in the Great Court to use the special computers that are connected to the new system called COMPASS. This is a huge interactive guide with information about thousands of objects in the British Museum. You can look up particular objects, make

The oldest objects in the Museum's collections are stone tools made 1.8 million years ago. The tools were found at Olduvai Gorge in Tanzania in the 1930s. They were an archaeological discovery of great significance because they suggested that early humans originated in Africa.

a souvenir of your visit and even print out a map with the objects' locations marked on it. If you are connected to the Internet you can use COMPASS at home to plan a visit, get help with a school project, or just for fun. Look out for the special children's area of COMPASS that will feature favourite objects, special children's tours and fun activities.

Look inside the back cover for useful British Museum information, phone numbers and our website address.

British Museum archaeologists carefully excavate a hoard of gold torcs (neck-rings) at Snettisham in Suffolk.

Most galleries in the British Museum concentrate on a particular period or culture, but the HSBC Money Gallery looks at currency in different countries and at different times.

Ideas to help you enjoy your visit

☞ Choose a few areas to look at and give yourself enough time really to take them in.
☞ Look at objects from different angles.
☞ Bring a notebook and pencil and draw the objects that interest you.
☞ Choose a few objects that you like and find out about them. Who made them, and why? What happened to the objects over time? Do we have anything like them today?
☞ Look for things that are similar.
☞ Look for things that are different.
☞ Can you find the oldest object in a gallery?
☞ Can you find the newest?

When you passed under the British Museum's famous entrance portico, you entered a magical world in which you can go back in time and travel around the globe. Like the millions of people who have visited this remarkable temple to curiosity and imagination, you will be filled with wonder at the amazing, beautiful and sometimes peculiar objects to be seen here. Welcome to the wonderful world of the British Museum!

The artist Alfred Stevens designed the cast-iron lion that guarded the Museum's boundaries until 1896. The lion image is still used to represent the British Museum.

I'll point out how my museum works as we travel through time and around the globe. Let's go!

Ancient Egypt

The spectacular achievements of the ancient Egyptians more than 5,000 years ago all depended on the River Nile. The Nile begins in the mountains of tropical Africa where rainfall is plentiful. Every year the river flooded its banks as it passed through the desert plains of Egypt. The farmers of ancient Egypt were able to grow crops and raise animals on the rich soil the water left behind and so the country grew rich and powerful.

◄ This stone holds the key that unlocked the secrets of the lost language of ancient Egypt. French soldiers discovered the stone in the Egyptian town of Rosetta in 1799. The Rosetta Stone is carved with the same text in three different scripts: hieroglyphs, another form of Egyptian writing called demotic, and Greek. The French scholar Jean-François Champollion worked out that the oval rings (called cartouches) contained royal names. Then he went on to decipher ancient Egyptian writing and prove that most hieroglyphs represented sounds.

Don't forget to look at the back of statues. Try to work out whether they were made to be free-standing or to be placed against a wall.

▲ The ancient Egyptian pharaohs built magnificent temples and carved huge stone statues. The pharaoh Rameses II ruled for sixty-seven years. He put up more statues of himself than any other pharaoh. This head comes from a pair of massive seated figures of Rameses. They stood inside the temple we now call the Ramesseum. This statue was carved from a single piece of granite in two colours. You can see how the sculptors used the colours to distinguish between the head and the body.

► The Nile was also home to many fish, birds and wild animals, which people hunted for food and sport. This tomb painting shows an official called Nebamun out hunting wild birds in the Nile marshes with his wife, daughter and cat.

◀ Travelling by land was difficult in the hills and deserts of ancient Egypt, so the River Nile was the main means of transport. Boats were used in many aspects of daily life and they also carried the dead on their funeral voyage. Under the canopy of this model lies a mummy attended by a priest and mourners.

▶ The ancient Egyptians believed that people would enjoy eternal life in the next world if their bodies were preserved after death. The ancient Egyptians became very skilled at mummification. With modern technology, curators can look inside mummies without damaging them. So curators can build up a picture of what individual people really looked like. The mask of this mummy shows Katebet as a beautiful young woman, but the X-ray reveals that she was old when she died and had only two teeth left!

◀ The ancient Egyptians wore amulets and charms to protect them from evil. They also tucked amulets inside mummies' linen bandages to protect the dead on their journey to the next world. Thousands of amulets have been found in Egyptian tombs and you can see lots of different types in the British Museum. This amulet combines the hieroglyphs for 'life' (pronounced *ankh*) with those meaning 'power', 'stability' and 'millions'. So the amulet represents a wish, probably for the king, of 'life, power and stability for millions of years'.

Ancient Greece

The ancient Greeks were proud of their culture. They would have been delighted to know that their accomplishments would inspire architects, sculptors, writers, thinkers and athletes of the western world for thousands of years. The British Museum has a fantastic collection of objects from every period of Greek civilization. There are world-famous works of art as well as everyday objects. Many vases, sculptures, coins and other objects illustrate scenes from Greek mythology, the vivid stories of gods, men and monsters that still have the power to grip our imagination.

◀ According to legend, King Minos lived at Knossos on the island of Crete. He kept a fierce monster called the Minotaur in a maze under the palace. The Minotaur was half-man and half-bull. Archaeologists found no trace of a maze nor of King Minos when they excavated the palace, but they did find lots of evidence that bulls were important in Minoan culture. This little bronze statue is of a boy (minus his legs) somersaulting between the horns of a charging bull. This dangerous sport was popular with the Minoans.

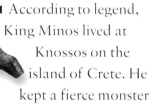

◀ Athens was the most powerful of the city-states that made up the ancient Greek world. The city took its name from Athena, the goddess of wisdom. Athena is often shown with her companion – a wise owl. For more than 300 years Athenian coins carried the head of the goddess on one side and her owl on the other.

▲ The painting on this vase illustrates a story about the Amazons, the women warriors who lived without men. The Amazons went to help the Trojans during their long battle to defend the city of Troy against the Greeks. This scene shows the Amazon Queen Penthesilea. She is being defeated in battle by Achilles, the greatest of the Greek warriors. According to one version of the story, the eyes of the two warriors met at the very moment when Achilles' spear was driving into her throat. Tragically, they fell instantly in love. Exekias, the potter who made and decorated this vase, signed his name just behind Achilles' right arm.

Everyday things are just as important as great works of art in helping us understand the past.

▼ In ancient Greece wealthy people had plenty of leisure time and many ways to amuse themselves. This little terracotta statue is of two women playing knucklebones, a game that was similar to jacks. Players threw the knucklebones into the air and then tried to catch them on the backs of their hands. A classical writer said that it was a game mostly played by women.

▲ This grand structure is the tomb of a powerful man. He died in the country of Lykia (now south-western Turkey) about 380 BC. The building had fallen down, perhaps in an earthquake, long before the pieces were brought to England. The British Museum cannot be completely sure that all the segments have been put back in the right place! However, most people agree that the three wind-blown figures represent Nereids, daughters of the seagods Nereus and Doris, so the building is known as the Nereid Monument.

▼ About 2,500 years ago the citizens of Athens built the great temple called the Parthenon in honour of Athena. The Parthenon was decorated with a carved frieze showing pictures of a great procession. This took place every four years to celebrate Athena's birthday. The marble blocks show riders on horses, chariots and people bearing sacrificial offerings. The frieze was originally painted, but the colours have faded. You can still see the holes where the horses' bronze bridles were attached.

The Roman Empire

At the end of the first century AD the Roman empire was at its largest. It covered most of Europe, North Africa and parts of the Middle East. The Roman emperors were able to control this vast multicultural empire because they had an extremely efficient system of governing the people they conquered and a highly trained army. They made sure that the official languages, Latin and Greek, were used all over the empire and they built an excellent network of roads that encouraged people to trade and communicate. They allowed people to keep their own religions and customs as long as they did not challenge the ultimate authority of Rome.

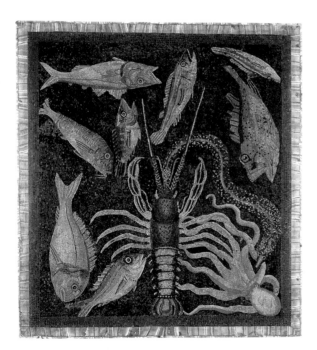

▲ This mosaic floor panel comes from the dining room of a Roman villa in Italy. It shows some of the edible fish of the Mediterranean region of the empire. Roman villas were very colourful places. Floors were often decorated with brightly coloured mosaics like this and the walls and ceilings were covered with vivid paintings.

▲ Emperor Hadrian travelled all over his vast empire studying its cultures and peoples and fortifying its borders. He built an eighty-mile-long wall across the north of Britain to keep out the 'barbarians', the people who were not under Roman rule. Hadrian came to Britain in AD 122 and this bronze head may come from a statue put up in honour of his visit. It was found in the River Thames near London Bridge in 1834. Hadrian was the first Roman emperor to have a beard and he made beards popular all over the empire.

In the past, museums sometimes added bits that were missing to sculptures when they were restored. However, today most objects are displayed as they were found, nose or no nose!

◄ Every important town throughout the Roman empire had an amphitheatre where crowds gathered to watch gladiators and wild animals fight to the death. Professional gladiators trained in special schools. The heavily armed *murmillo* gladiators wore bronze helmets that enclosed and protected the face and neck.

▼ This young man lived in Egypt, the most southerly part of the Roman empire. When he died his body was mummified and his mummy case was painted with traditional Egyptian funerary scenes. But his family may originally have been Greek, because 'Farewell Artemidorus' is written in Greek on the mummy case. (The word 'farewell' has been spelled wrongly, which could mean that the writer's Greek was getting rusty!) Artemidorus has a Roman hairstyle and his portrait has been painted in the realistic Roman style.

▲ Roman soldiers often took their families with them when they were stationed far from home. These thin pieces of wood are letters and they give us a glimpse of what life was like for the soldiers and their relatives in the Roman fort of Vindolanda, near Hadrian's Wall. Claudia Severa has written to her friend Sulpicia Lepidina, asking her to a birthday party. She says: 'I give you a warm invitation to make sure that you come to us, and make the day more enjoyable for me by your arrival.'

◄ The Romans treated wild animals in a way that we would consider quite cruel. However, they were very fond of the animals they kept as pets. This sculpture of two greyhounds was found in the eighteenth century in the ruins of a Roman villa in Italy. There is a faint mark around the neck of the female, so she may once have worn a metal collar.

Objects from the Roman empire are in Rooms 23, 49, 69–73, 77, 78, 83–85 and on the North Stairs

The Ancient Near East

About the middle of the fourth millennium BC the first cities in the world were created in the fertile land of Mesopotamia, which is the region between the Tigris and Euphrates rivers, in modern Iraq. People had to work together in large communities to make sure the crops were irrigated and collections of buildings grew up on the banks of the great rivers. The largest and most important buildings in the cities were temples. People brought food and precious goods to the temples to offer to the gods. The picture-like symbols used to keep an account of temple deliveries later developed into cuneiform, probably the earliest system of writing in the world.

◀ Cuneiform was written by pressing the end of a cut reed into a moist clay surface. Cuneiform means 'wedge-shaped'. This clay tablet contains a unique map. At the centre is Babylon on the River Euphrates. Mesopotamia itself is ringed by a circular waterway labelled 'salt sea' and this is surrounded by triangles labelled 'region' or 'island'. The cuneiform text names the strange beasts and heroes that were believed to live there. Even though the places are roughly in their correct positions, the map is not really an example of ancient geography. It shows how Babylonians pictured their mythological world.

▲ This massive human-headed winged bull is one of a pair that once guarded an entrance to the palace built by the Assyrian King Sargon II in the eighth century BC. The sculptors roughly shaped the huge blocks of marble while they were still in the quarry. Then they moved the sculptures to the palace and finished them off. The bulls weigh about sixteen tonnes each and they are among the heaviest objects in the British Museum. The bulls were designed to be viewed from the side as well as the front, which is the reason why they each have five legs.

Keep an eye out for different ways of writing as you travel round the Museum.

► The Oxus Treasure was discovered in 1880 near the River Oxus in Central Asia. This magnificent hoard of gold and silver is one of the Museum's greatest treasures. The hoard passed through the hands of bandits and merchants who mixed up objects from different periods and places. This makes it difficult to work out exactly where the pieces came from. One of the finest pieces is this little gold model of a chariot pulled by four horses. The seated passenger is much larger than the charioteer, which probably means he was a person of high rank.

◄ About 1200 BC the Egyptian empire was attacked by the 'Sea Peoples', who might have come from present-day Greece and Turkey. The Egyptians defeated them and one group, known as the Philistines, settled on the coast at Canaan. Like the Egyptians, the Philistines buried their dead in coffins with human faces, although Philistine coffins are made of clay. Archaeologists have found some Philistine coffins with hieroglyphs written on them. However, the inscriptions do not make sense, perhaps because the person who wrote them was just copying the symbols and did not understand the language.

► When archaeologists excavated the Sumerian city of Ur in the 1920s, they found an amazingly rich collection of jewellery, weapons, armour and musical instruments buried in the graves of the ancient kings and queens. Among the spectacular objects were several versions of this board game, which is now known as the Royal Game of Ur. Two players threw dice and moved their counters around a decorated board of twenty squares. This game was extremely popular throughout the Middle East for centuries.

The Islamic World and Central Asia

For followers of Islam, known as Muslims, the holy book called the Qur'an (sometimes written Koran) contains the word of God as told to the Prophet Muhammad. The Prophet lived in Arabia in the seventh century. The word Islam means 'submission', and Muslims acknowledge loyalty and obedience to God and his messenger Muhammad. There are no priests in Islam, although there are religious scholars and an imam to lead the prayers in most mosques. Islam has spread far beyond its Arab origins and there are now millions of Muslims throughout Asia, Africa, Europe and North America.

▲ Many Islamic buildings are decorated with brilliantly coloured tiles with patterns based on geometric shapes like the circle, triangle and square. These shapes are pleasing to look at and they also have symbolic meanings in Islamic culture. The circle represents the great arch of the sky. The square represents the four directions of earth. Other designs are based on plants and flowers.

▶ The words of the Qur'an are sacred to Muslims so the art of writing, called calligraphy, has always been highly valued in the Islamic world. Beautiful writing was often used to decorate coins, pottery and buildings, particularly those with a religious purpose. Many Muslims would not allow images of people and animals in mosques. They thought that this was trying to outdo the creative powers of God. The contemporary Egyptian calligrapher Ahmed Mustafa made this print of a chapter of the Qur'an.

▲ Astrolabes were stunning scientific instruments that were used throughout the Middle Ages. The ancient Greeks invented the astrolabe, but it was Muslim astronomers who developed it. With an astrolabe people could use the position of the sun to tell the time during the day, and the stars to tell the time at night. This was very important in the Islamic world because Muslims need to pray five times each day. People also used astrolabes for astrological purposes and to try and find out what the future held in store for them.

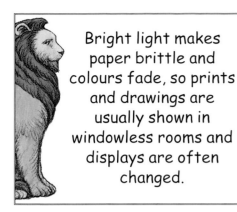

Bright light makes paper brittle and colours fade, so prints and drawings are usually shown in windowless rooms and displays are often changed.

◄ The women of Palestine made beautiful costumes to wear on special occasions. They decorated the clothes with rich embroidery and patchwork. The colour of the fabric, the type of stitching and the way the belt or veil was worn said a lot about the wearer. They showed whether a woman was married, where she came from and how wealthy she was. Elaborate headdresses and jewellery made of metal coins and precious stones also indicated a person's wealth.

▲ The people who live in Central Asia have traditionally led a nomadic way of life, herding animals in the high mountain steppes. In the winter Kyrgyz women make felt from sheep's wool. Felt is a waterproof and warm fabric that can be used for many purposes. Women get together to create bright 'mosaic' floor coverings, sitting with their legs under the felt for warmth while they sew. Sheets of white felt are dyed, cut into shapes and fitted together like patchwork. Some of the patterns used today are over 2,500 years old.

▶ There is an old Islamic tradition of using figures in books. In the sixteenth and seventeenth centuries the rulers of Iran and India appointed court artists to produce beautiful miniature paintings that told stories of kings and heroes. In this picture a royal picnic is taking place at night. The prince, who is wearing an elaborate fur-lined jacket, is waited on by servants and entertained by female musicians. The man wearing a turban in the foreground is offering a cup of wine to the women, who seem to be laughing at him.

Japan, China and Korea

The countries of East Asia have greatly influenced one another over many centuries, but each has followed its own distinctive path and created a unique civilization and culture. Buddhism is the most important religion throughout the region, but has developed in quite different ways in China, Japan and Korea. And although each of these countries has been isolated at times in the past, today they have a significant influence on the rest of the world. The traditions of their ancestors are still very important to people of East Asia. They combine respect for the past with the most advanced technologies.

◄ No theatre has been performed in Japan since the Middle Ages. It is still popular today. Players move slowly on the stage to the accompaniment of hypnotic music from the drum and flute. Many of the performers wear masks, so gesture is often used to indicate emotions. Touching the sleeve can suggest happiness in love; raising the right hand means weeping. This painted and lacquered wooden mask represents Hannya, a beautiful woman who was transformed into a devil by jealousy.

▲ Samurai first served as bodyguards at the imperial Japanese court. As the power of the emperor diminished samurai became powerful leaders in their own right. Throughout the eleventh and twelfth centuries, samurai fought one another for control of Japan. This magnificent suit of samurai armour consists of pieces made between the seventeenth and nineteenth centuries. By then, samurai wore armour for display rather than warfare. Samurai were not just fierce warriors. They were expected also to be men of culture who appreciated poetry and art.

▶ Tigers are native to Asia, but they do not live in the wild in Japan. Japanese artists were fascinated by tigers, but they had to use the skins of dead animals as models. The eighteenth-century artist Ganku became famous for his tiger paintings. He has painted the animal with care while the tree, rocks and water are painted in a much freer, bolder style.

◄ The rest of the world recognized many centuries ago that the Chinese were experts at turning clay into beautiful objects. Chinese blue-and-white porcelain is famous, but most of it was not made for Chinese people to use. The porcelain was exported overseas, particularly to Islamic countries. The shape of this fourteenth-century dish is inspired by Islamic metalwork, although the design of flowers and a fish swimming among waterweeds is very Chinese.

► The earliest Chinese coins looked very different from the coins used today. Some bronze coins were made in the shape of tools like knives and hoes, and their value was based on the weight of the metal. This knife-shaped coin was made by casting, a technique in which molten metal is poured into a mould and then allowed to cool.

► Horses and camels carried luxury goods along the great Central Asian trading route called the Silk Road. Chinese goods were traded far afield, and foreign goods and ideas came back to China. During the Tang dynasty (AD 618–906) China was particularly open to outside influences. When a person died, ceramic objects were buried in the tomb. The objects represented everything the dead person needed to carry on a normal life in the afterworld. The many figures of horses and camels found in Tang tombs show the importance of these animals at the time.

The colours in glazed pottery do not fade, unlike those in textiles, drawings and paintings.

► Archaeologists have excavated royal Korean tombs from the Silla dynasty (fifth–sixth centuries AD). They have found many magnificent golden objects – crowns, belts, earrings, necklaces and even shoes! The precious metal was beaten with a hammer to make a thin sheet. Then craftsmen cut it into shapes and joined them together with twisted gold wire. These gold earrings were not for pierced ears. They were hung from a string tied around the ear. The custom of wearing earrings is thought to have reached Korea from China. The Chinese wore glass earrings, but the Koreans introduced gold ones in the fourth century AD.

India, South Asia and South-East Asia

Ever since human beings first felt a sense of wonder about their world, they have searched for a meaning and purpose in life. Many people have found that religion provides an answer to these important questions. Hinduism and Buddhism originated in the northern part of the Indian subcontinent and still play a significant part in the lives of millions of Asians. Most Hindus live in India, although Buddhism and Islam have spread throughout the region. Other beliefs centred on ancestors and the spirit world exist in parts of South-East Asia.

◀ A Hindu temple is seen as the earthly house of a god. Some worshippers recite prayers, read the scriptures or bring offerings of flowers and food to the temple every day. Other people might employ a priest to do this on their behalf, and visit the temple only for festivals. Hindus sometimes made a contribution to places of worship and pilgrimage by donating a model of a miniature temple like this.

▲ Shadow puppet plays are a popular form of theatre in Java (now part of Indonesia). The puppets are held up against a white sheet. A light behind them casts a shadow on the screen in front of the audience. The shadow puppets are made from dried animal hide that is cut and pierced to allow light to pass through. Many plays are based on the Hindu epic the Ramayana, and describe Rama's struggle against the forces of evil.

▶ According to the Hindu story, the god Shiva cut off Ganesha's head in a rage. Ganesha's mother Parvati pleaded with Shiva to restore her son's head. Shiva promised that he would replace it with that of the first creature he came across, which happened to be an elephant. In this sculpture Ganesha has five heads and ten arms. He is sitting beneath a tree holding various weapons in his ten hands. His wife sits on one knee and his companion, a rat, crouches under his foot.

The Iban people of Sarawak in the north-west of Borneo used to call on one of their gods when they went on head-hunting raids against enemy villages. The deity Singalang Burong was invited to inhabit this magnificent carving of a rhinoceros hornbill. The carving would have been erected on a tall pole outside the longhouse facing in the direction of the enemy's territory. In a special ceremony the raiders would ask the god to weaken their opponents before the attack.

▶ The great religious teacher Buddha was born Prince Siddhartha in the sixth century BC. He gave up his privileged life in order to help others escape from suffering and the endless cycle of rebirth. The story of Buddha's search for enlightenment was recorded in the third century BC on a stone frieze carved in Gandhara, the ancient name for the north-western part of Pakistan. This panel shows Buddha on his deathbed surrounded by his grieving followers, at the moment when he achieves nirvana.

Gods, kings or queens are often shown larger than other people as a way of indicating their importance.

◀ The cycle-rickshaws of Bangladesh are like travelling art exhibitions. The frames, hoods and seats are elaborately decorated in brilliant colours. Rickshaws are the most common form of transport in Dhaka, the capital of Bangladesh. Many Bangladeshis today depend on the rickshaw industry to earn a living.

Africa

People have flourished on the vast and varied continent of Africa for about two million years. The ancient Egyptians built a highly developed society on the banks of the River Nile, and archaeologists have found evidence of cities and other sophisticated early civilizations throughout the continent. Trade with people from Europe and Asia has contributed to the cultural diversity of Africa over the centuries. Africans too have travelled throughout the world, particularly as a result of being taken as slaves to the Americas. Many Africans had their own kingdoms and empires, but in the nineteenth century European countries created the boundaries of the African nations that exist today.

◀ In most parts of Africa, making pottery is women's work. The pots are made by hand rather than on a wheel. This pot from southern Africa was made by coiling long, thin sausages of clay to build up the shape. After the clay had dried, the pot was fired in a carefully prepared bonfire. Pots like these were used for storing and drinking beer. The lid, which is much more recent, uses traditional basketry techniques but is made with telephone wire.

▲ The thick tropical forests of central Africa provided the Kuba people with hardwood that they used for beautiful carvings. This carving is of Shyaam-a-Mbul Ngwoong, the seventeenth-century Kuba king who founded the kingdom. He introduced his people to mancala, the game that is played on the board in front of him. Mancala is still a popular game in Africa and many other parts of the world.

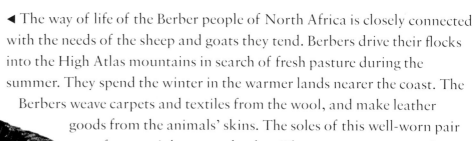

◀ The way of life of the Berber people of North Africa is closely connected with the needs of the sheep and goats they tend. Berbers drive their flocks into the High Atlas mountains in search of fresh pasture during the summer. They spend the winter in the warmer lands nearer the coast. The Berbers weave carpets and textiles from the wool, and make leather goods from the animals' skins. The soles of this well-worn pair of women's boots are leather. The upper parts are made from fabric, woven to the shape of the boots.

◄ The wealth of the Asante kingdom in nineteenth-century Ghana was based on the gold trade. The Asante king and chiefs still wear spectacular amounts of gold on ceremonial occasions. This chief is wearing a gold headpiece, rings, bracelets and necklace and his attendants carry ceremonial swords with golden hilts. The Asante goldsmiths were masters of 'lost-wax' casting and they could produce very intricate and delicate objects. Asante weavers made the *kente* cloth that the chief is wearing. They wove long narrow strips of cloth and sewed them together.

▶ The leather base of this Ethiopian shield is covered with velvet imported from India and decorative silver pieces made from melted-down coins from Austria. Fixed to the centre is the mane of a lion, the royal beast of Ethiopia. The mane shows that the shield's owner was a person of high rank who had won honour in battle. During the eighteenth and nineteenth centuries, the emperors of Ethiopia presented shields like these to their regional governors. A young man would stand behind the governor and hold up the shield as he spoke, so that everyone could see at a glance how important the governor was.

▼ This brass plaque was made to decorate the wooden pillars of the magnificent palace compound of the Oba, the king of the city-state of Benin in Nigeria. The plaque shows two of the Oba's soldiers in front of the palace building. On either side are two young men, probably sons of chiefs sent to serve the king. They were not allowed to wear clothes until they became adults.

When traders and settlers travelled across the world, they introduced others to their beliefs, and their ways of decorating and making objects.

Objects from Africa are in Room 25 ⑲

The Americas

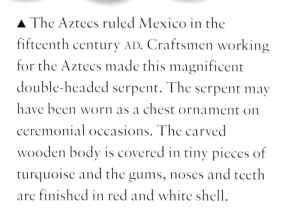

Archaeologists believe that the first people to discover the Americas were Siberian hunters, who walked across to Alaska during the last Ice Age, more than 14,000 years ago. As they slowly spread through North and South America over the years, they developed different cultures and ways of living. Some peoples of Central and South America began to grow crops, and farming spread to parts of North America. Other peoples continued to live by hunting and gathering. When people from Europe and Africa arrived, from the sixteenth century onwards, they brought new ways of life and eventually took control of both continents.

▲ The Aztecs ruled Mexico in the fifteenth century AD. Craftsmen working for the Aztecs made this magnificent double-headed serpent. The serpent may have been worn as a chest ornament on ceremonial occasions. The carved wooden body is covered in tiny pieces of turquoise and the gums, noses and teeth are finished in red and white shell.

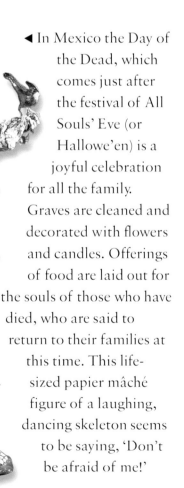

◀ In Mexico the Day of the Dead, which comes just after the festival of All Souls' Eve (or Hallowe'en) is a joyful celebration for all the family. Graves are cleaned and decorated with flowers and candles. Offerings of food are laid out for the souls of those who have died, who are said to return to their families at this time. This life-sized papier mâché figure of a laughing, dancing skeleton seems to be saying, 'Don't be afraid of me!'

▼ The Maya people of Central America had a sophisticated system of writing that they used to record important events in the lives of their rulers. This beautifully carved panel is a door lintel. It comes from a building in the magnificent Maya city of Yaxchilan and shows the eighth-century king Bird Jaguar. The king stands over a captured nobleman who has just given blood. At some public events and to ensure success in battle the Maya performed rituals in which they made themselves bleed.

▲ Some Native North Americans used shells called *wampum* as currency. In time, European settlers in North America began to create their own paper money. Printed banknotes were convenient, but were easy to copy. This one shilling note was printed in New Jersey in 1776 by Benjamin Franklin. He invented a special process called 'nature printing' to make it difficult for people to forge money. Franklin made plaster casts of real leaves and used these to create unique printing plates.

▶ Europeans came to North America in the sixteenth century, searching for wealth and new lands to colonize. There were already between two and five million native people living there. Colonists recorded native peoples' way of life in words and pictures, which they sent back to Europe along with furs and other valuables. John White copied this portrait of a Timucua woman from Florida. You can see the tattoos that covered her body and face. She is wearing a garment made of moss. It was probably not really as blue as it has been painted.

When the British Museum collects objects made by living people, curators try to find out as much as possible about what they mean to their makers.

◀ The people of the far north could not survive the freezing temperatures and harsh climate of the Arctic without their beautifully designed clothing. This is a traditional garment of the Inuit people. It is a young girl's caribou-fur parka. For warmth, it was worn over a second parka that had the fur turned to the inside. Air was trapped inside each hollow hair and more was caught between the layers, so the wearer was well insulated from the cold outside. The hood may have had a longer fringe of wolf fur, to enable snow and ice to be shaken off easily.

Objects from The Americas are in Rooms 26, 27 (banknote in 68)

The Pacific Islands and Australia

The scattered islands of the vast Pacific Ocean were settled over thousands of years by voyagers whose ancestors came originally from South-East Asia. The settlers lived by farming, foraging in the forests and fishing. They had much in common, but there were also many cultural differences between peoples. War between neighbours was not unusual.

For more than 50,000 years Aborigines lived by hunting and gathering on the Australian continent. They illustrated their deep relationship with the land in paintings on rock and bark. The paintings produced by modern Aboriginal painters on canvas are collected by art galleries and museums around the world.

▶ In many parts of Papua New Guinea, people would hold great festivals, when spirits were supposed to visit the village and make sure that life went on just as it should. The spirits appeared as masks, like this one from the southern coast of Papua New Guinea. The man wearing the mask would be almost completely hidden. Only his legs showed under the leaf skirt. Women and children were not supposed to know that the masks were made and worn by their own menfolk.

◀ Captain Cook made three voyages to the Pacific between 1768 and 1780. Cook's voyages provided Europeans with a huge amount of new knowledge about the people, plants and animals of the southern hemisphere. A young artist called William Hodges accompanied Cook on his second voyage. Hodges drew this picture of the island of Tahiti. Scenes like this made people in Europe think that the Pacific islands were paradise on earth.

Objects made from plant and animal materials were rarely intended to last a very long time and the Museum needs to take special care to preserve them for the future.

► Like other Pacific islanders, the Maori people of New Zealand consider tattoos very attractive. Men and women's bodies are often decorated in this way. Tattooing is a painful process, so a tattoo is also lifelong proof of courage. A person undergoing a facial tattoo drank broth or water from funnels like this one. The funnels were carved with very elaborate designs. These may have been a way of distracting the person from the pain.

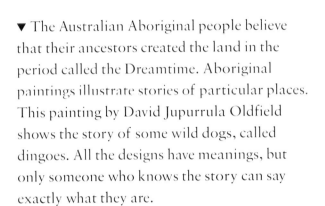

▼ The Australian Aboriginal people believe that their ancestors created the land in the period called the Dreamtime. Aboriginal paintings illustrate stories of particular places. This painting by David Jupurrula Oldfield shows the story of some wild dogs, called dingoes. All the designs have meanings, but only someone who knows the story can say exactly what they are.

▲ This chest pendant from Solomon Islands is made from a ring that has been fashioned from clam shell. It is backed with carved turtleshell and has been ornamented with glass beads, porpoise teeth and shirt buttons. In Solomon Islands, as in some other Pacific Islands countries, valuable objects like shell rings and beads are given for important exchanges such as marriage, and may also be made into ornaments. This one would have been worn by an important person such as a clan leader or chief.

Prehistory and Early Europe

Most of the 800,000 or so years that have passed since human beings first arrived in Europe from Africa are known as prehistory, which means 'before writing'. The prehistoric era is usually divided into the Stone, Bronze and Iron Ages after the materials used to make tools at the time. The Roman conquest brought an end to the prehistoric period in much of Europe and for about 500 years the region was united under one empire. After the collapse of Roman civilization, outsiders from the north and east fought to establish their own kingdoms and people were often at war with their neighbours. This period is sometimes called the Dark Ages, even though magnificent objects survive from this time and show that there was still a sophisticated culture in Europe.

▲ People were living in the north of England about 9,000 years ago, not long after the end of the last Ice Age. They survived largely by collecting plant foods and by hunting animals such as deer and elk. These large mammals provided humans with meat and skins and their antlers were used to make tools. This rare headdress is made from the skull and antlers of a red deer stag. It might have been attached to a leather hood. Hunters might have worn it when stalking their prey.

◄ Six thousand years ago the early farmers living in the south of England were making complex structures like this timber trackway to help them to walk over marshy land. They prepared the track on dry land from the wood of oak, ash, lime, hazel and alder trees. Then they assembled the track on site. Even though the whole track is nearly two kilometres long, it could be put together in a single day. By studying the tree rings, scientists have been able to work out that the track was made in either 3807 or 3806 BC.

▼ Prehistoric people discovered that copper and tin could be combined to make bronze. They could make completely new types of objects from bronze because it was so strong. This bronze 'flesh hook' was used to lift lumps of cooked meat out of a cauldron. It is decorated with a family of swans and a pair of ravens marching towards each other. The flesh hook was made in Ireland between 950 and 750 BC.

◀ This shield looks magnificent, but it was made for show and not for battle. Shields used for fighting were made out of wood. This shield, with its polished metal and swirling pattern, must have made a big impression 2,000 years ago. It was probably a ritual offering thrown into the River Thames, where it stayed until it was dredged out near Battersea Bridge in 1857.

▶ This man met a violent death about the time the Romans arrived in England, in the middle of the first century AD. A couple of blows from a heavy object smashed his skull, then he was strangled with a thin cord. This probably killed him, but just to make sure, his throat was cut before he was dropped face down into a peat bog. It is possible that he was a sacrificial victim, rather than just the unlucky victim of an attack. Lindow Man (who is sometimes affectionately known as 'Pete Marsh') was found in 1984 when workmen cutting peat sliced through his body.

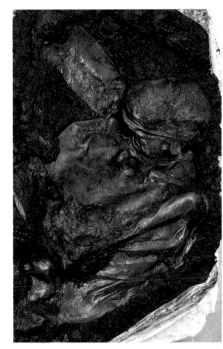

◀ In troubled times wealthy people often tried to hide their valuables by burying them in the ground and sometimes they didn't return to dig them up. In 1992 a rich hoard of treasure from Roman Britain was discovered in Suffolk, England. It was one of the largest ever found. The Hoxne hoard consisted of nearly 15,000 coins and many other precious objects, buried for safety in the fifth century AD.

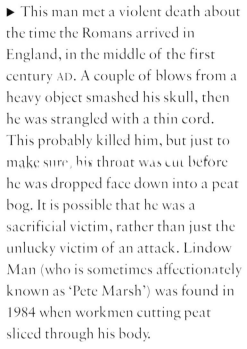

▶ The dramatic discovery of the Sutton Hoo burial site in Suffolk in 1939 completely transformed archaeologists' understanding of Anglo-Saxon Britain. Great mounds of earth were excavated to reveal the remains of a seventh-century wooden ship. An Anglo-Saxon king had been buried in the ship with his splendid weapons, treasure and ornaments. Many of the beautiful and intricate objects survived intact, although the king's helmet had to be carefully reconstructed out of more than 500 fragments.

Europe during the Middle Ages and the Renaissance

The twelfth and thirteenth centuries were a period of growth and expansion in Europe. Great cities developed and the population increased. The Christian Church was more powerful than most monarchs during the Middle Ages. The Church used its fabulous riches to build cathedrals and commission works of art to the glory of God. But by the fifteenth century people were taking a new interest in classical learning and they began to question traditional beliefs. The wonderful works of art produced during the Renaissance (which is the French for 'rebirth') are some of the most famous in the world.

▲ These chessmen look puzzled – rather like the people who have tried to solve the mystery that surrounds them. To this day, no one knows who carved the ninety-three little figures out of walrus-tusk ivory and no one knows how they got to the Isle of Lewis in the Outer Hebrides where they were found in 1831. One theory is that the chessmen may have belonged to a twelfth-century Scandinavian trader who was shipwrecked and the pieces were washed ashore. Some of the pieces were once stained red, but the colour has long since worn off.

▲ Fragments of bone or objects associated with holy people and events have a special significance to believers. Medieval Christians made elaborate containers for these precious relics. This portrait head was made about AD 1200 for the Cathedral of Basle in Switzerland. It was made to hold a relic of the skull of St Eustace, a Roman soldier who converted to Christianity.

▶ Italian Renaissance potters invented a new kind of glazed pottery, called *maiolica*, which enabled them to paint detailed pictures in brilliant colours. Wealthy patrons commissioned artists to illustrate stories from classical mythology and history on bowls and dishes. The colours on these objects are still as bright as when they were first made.

◀ The great Renaissance artist Leonardo da Vinci (1452–1519) was also a brilliant scientist and engineer. Leonardo was intensely curious about the world. Over his lifetime he filled his notebooks with thousands of drawings and made many important scientific discoveries. Leonardo made this drawing when he was still a young man studying in Florence. It shows how he noted every tiny detail. Nobody knows for sure who this stern soldier was.

◀ The defeat of the Spanish Armada in 1588 by the smaller, swifter ships of the English navy was a great triumph for Queen Elizabeth I. This ornate gold medal was made about the time of the Armada. It may well have been a gift from the queen herself to a favourite courtier. The medal was designed by Nicholas Hilliard, who is best known as a painter of miniature portraits.

◀ The powerful rulers of Europe spent fortunes keeping themselves entertained. This elaborate model of a galleon (called a nef) tells the time! It has a spectacular way of announcing the start of a banquet. The ship moves along the table, rocking and rolling as if at sea, while a tiny organ below deck plays a tune. Drummers and trumpeters play, and the courtiers move in a procession around the Holy Roman Emperor's throne. The sailors in the crows' nests strike the hours and quarter-hours. Cannons are fired at the end of the performance. The clock itself is hard to see, tucked away at the foot of the mainmast.

Objects from Europe during the Middle Ages and Renaissance are in Rooms 41-44 and 46

Europe since the Renaissance

In the sixteenth and seventeenth centuries the population in Europe was growing at a dramatic rate. At the same time, struggles between Catholics and Protestants were creating religious refugees. Europeans sailed all over the world looking for new lands to colonize, trading everything from slaves to spices. Great advances in science and engineering took place during the eighteenth and nineteenth centuries and the Industrial Revolution transformed the lives of most people in Europe. The twentieth century brought technological advances beyond our ancestors' wildest dreams. The rate of change shows no sign of slowing down in the twenty-first century.

▲ This magnificent clock still goes for a whole year on one winding. It was made in 1689 for King William III by the master clockmaker Thomas Tompion. When a little cord at the side was pulled the clock struck the most recent hour and quarter-hour, so the king could tell the time even in the middle of the night. The figure of Britannia stands over silver symbols of the rose of England, the thistle of Scotland and the royal emblems, the lion and the unicorn.

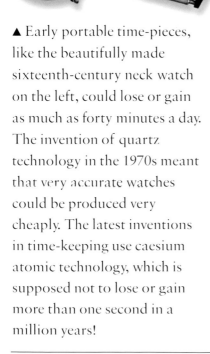

▲ Early portable time-pieces, like the beautifully made sixteenth-century neck watch on the left, could lose or gain as much as forty minutes a day. The invention of quartz technology in the 1970s meant that very accurate watches could be produced very cheaply. The latest inventions in time-keeping use caesium atomic technology, which is supposed not to lose or gain more than one second in a million years!

◄ The scene on this grand vase was inspired by ancient Greek art. It shows the poet Homer being honoured by a *nike*, a winged figure of victory. Homer holds a *kithara*, a musical instrument that ancient Greeks played to accompany lyric poetry. The vase is called the Pegasus Vase, after the winged horse on the lid. It was given to the British Museum in 1786 by Josiah Wedgwood, who owned the factory that made it.

► The artist William Hogarth (1697–1764) is famous for the prints he made about eighteenth-century life. 'Gin Lane' is set in a London street in Bloomsbury just before the British Museum was founded in 1753. At that time there was a craze for drinking gin, which was very cheap and widely available. Hogarth was trying to warn people of the dangers of drinking gin. The woman in the centre is too drunk to notice that her baby has fallen down the steps. Another mother is tipping gin into her baby's mouth.

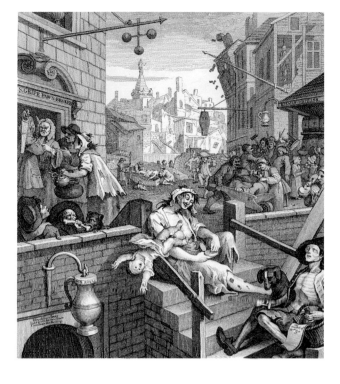

◄ At the ripe old age of seventy-two Mrs Mary Delany invented a way of making incredibly realistic collage pictures of flowers. She called them 'paper mosaicks'. What appear at first glance to be pressed flowers and leaves are made from hundreds of tiny pieces of coloured paper stuck together. Eighteenth-century explorers like Captain Cook were bringing new and exotic plant species back to England, and there was a great deal of interest in botany at the time.

Several departments in the British Museum collect modern objects, so people in the future can get a picture of our way of life. Imagine you are visiting the British Museum a hundred years from now. What do you think you might see there?

► Credit cards began in America in the 1920s. Oil companies and hotels issued the cards to trustworthy customers to pay for petrol and hotel rooms. Today, plastic cards are often used instead of coins and paper money. Modern technology means that funds can be moved electronically at great speed. But even though precious metals are no longer used as everyday currency, banks still issue 'gold', 'silver' and 'platinum' cards because they represent high value.

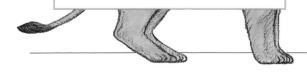

Objects from Europe since the Renaissance are in Rooms 44–48, 68, 90

The Story of The British Museum

There are many people who like to accumulate things, but few have had such a passion for collecting as Sir Hans Sloane. Sloane was a wealthy eighteenth-century doctor of great energy and curiosit who built up an enormous collection of objects over his lifetime. He crammed his house in Chelsea with all kinds of ancient relics, fossils, stuffed animals, plants, drawings, coins and rare books and he loved to show them to his guests. When Hans Sloane died in 1753, the government held a lottery to raise money to obtain his entire collection of more than 80,000 objects. This was the beginning of the British Museum.

A bust of Sir Hans Sloane, the founder of the British Museum, made in about 1737 by Michael Rysbrack.

The collection was moved to a grand house in Bloomsbury (which was then in green fields at the edge of London) and opened to visitors in 1759. For many years the Museum depended on gifts to build up the collections and everything that was received was written down in a 'Book of Presents'. Some of the stranger gifts included part of a tree gnawed by a beaver, a starved rat and even a dried thumb! Before long the rooms were jam-packed and the floors were beginning to sag. In the 1820s it was decided to create a new home for the Museum in a purpose-built building on the same site. It took thirty years to finish the grand building with its majestic entrance and almost at once it too began to fill up.

A drawing from the Illustrated London News *in the nineteenth century, called 'The Lost Tribe'. At closing time, lost children were collected at the foot of the main stairs of the Museum.*

A conservator works on the mummy mask of an Egyptian woman called Katebet.

On special occasions gallery staff wear a uniform that was originally designed for staff at Windsor Castle.

In the 1880s all the fossils, stuffed animals, rocks and plants were moved to new premises in South Kensington to become the Natural History Museum. The books, manuscripts, stamps and maps moved to the British Library's new building at St Pancras in the 1990s. Recently the builders have been in the Museum again, building the magnificent glass roof over the Great Court and creating more space for galleries and visitors.

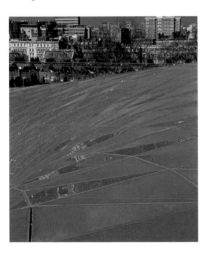

The new roof covering the Great Court contains 6,000 square metres of glass, enough to glaze 500 greenhouses.

More than 1,000 people work for the Museum today. They include curators, architects, administrators, cleaners, stonemasons, photographers, teachers, locksmiths and painters. Many of the staff work behind the scenes, although you will always see gallery staff in the public areas to help visitors find their way about and make sure the objects are safe.

Curators study the collections in their care, organize the displays in the galleries and plan exhibitions. They share their knowledge with other specialists and the public by writing information for the galleries, books and articles. There are ten curatorial departments, and the six million objects in the Museum are divided between them.

The Museum has several up-to-date laboratories. Scientists investigate how old things are and how they were made, using technology that does not harm the objects. Conservators ensure that objects are kept in good condition so that future generations will also be able to enjoy them. They check the instruments that record atmosphere, humidity and levels of pollution, and see that the environment in the galleries and display cases does not damage the objects.

The British Museum was supposed to be for any 'studious and curious person' who wanted to visit, but for the first fifty years visitors were not made to feel very welcome. They were not allowed to wander round on their own and for years people complained that the guided tours were so rushed that they had no time to look at the objects. Today, the British

More than five million people visited the British Museum in 1999.

Museum puts a great deal of effort into helping visitors to understand and appreciate the collections, and is happy for them to stay all day.

Every time you walk up the famous steps of the British Museum you enter a magical place where you can travel through time and around the world. You can visit every continent and find out about cultures that are different and similar, ancient and modern, near and far. We hope you enjoy visiting the amazing world of the British Museum and come back often.

QUIZ

Now you've been round the British Museum, test your knowledge about the objects you saw by doing this quiz. All the answers can be found in this book.

1. **An amulet is:**
   (a) a kind of ancient Egyptian temple
   (b) a token that provides protection from harm
   (c) a bracelet worn on the arm

2. **The ancient Greek goddess Athena's companion was:**
   (a) a dog, because she was loyal
   (b) a bee, because she worked hard
   (c) an owl, because she was wise

3. **Hadrian was the first Roman emperor to:**
   (a) wear a beard
   (b) wear trousers
   (c) wear an earring

4. **In ancient Mesopotamia, cuneiform was written by:**
   (a) dipping a feather in ink
   (b) scratching marks on stone with a metal point
   (c) pressing the end of a cut reed into clay

5. **Astrolabes were used to:**
   (a) tell the time
   (b) weigh precious metals
   (c) measure the amount of rainfall

6. **Early Chinese coins were made in the shape of:**
   (a) knives
   (b) forks
   (c) spoons

7. **The Hindu god Ganesha has the head of:**
   (a) a cat
   (b) an elephant
   (c) a cow

8. **In Africa, Ethiopian officials used their shields to:**
   (a) shade them from the sun
   (b) show how important they were
   (c) decorate their houses

9. **The Mexican festival of the Day of the Dead takes place at:**
   (a) Easter
   (b) Christmas
   (c) Hallowe'en

10. **The Maori people live in:**
    (a) Papua New Guinea
    (b) New Zealand
    (c) Solomon Islands

11. **Bronze is a metal made of:**
    (a) tin and copper
    (b) iron and copper
    (c) silver and copper

12. **Renaissance is a French word meaning:**
    (a) recycle
    (b) rebirth
    (c) receipt

13. **King William III had a special clock to:**
    (a) tell the time in the middle of the night
    (b) provide entertainment at dinnertime
    (c) work out how long it took to boil an egg

14. **The British Museum's collections once included:**
    (a) rocks and fossils
    (b) rare books and manuscripts
    (c) stuffed animals

© 2000 The Trustees of The British Museum

Published by British Museum Press
A division of The British Museum Company Ltd
46 Bloomsbury Street, London WC1B 3QQ

ISBN 0 7141 2727 2

A catalogue record for this book is available from the British Library

All the pictures of The British Museum Lion were drawn by Graham Percy.
Cover by Crayon Design, Henley-on-Thames.
Designed and typeset in Sabon by Margaret Sadler.
Printed in Hong Kong by Imago.